PRINCE WILLIAM & KATE

A Royal Romance

PRINCE WILLIAM & KATE

A Royal Romance

MATT DOEDEN

 LERNER PUBLICATIONS COMPANY · MINNEAPOLIS

Text copyright © 2012 by Lerner Publishing Group, Inc.

Lerner Publications Company
A division of Lerner Publishing Group, Inc.
241 First Avenue North
Minneapolis, MN 55401 U.S.A.

Website address: www.lernerbooks.com

Library of Congress Cataloging-in-Publication Data

Doeden, Matt.
    Prince William & Kate : a royal romance / By Matt Doeden.
        p.   cm. — (Gateway biographies)
    Includes bibliographical references and index.
    ISBN 978-0-7613-8029-0 (lib. bdg. : alk. paper)
    1. William, Prince, grandson of Elizabeth II, Queen of Great Britain, 1982—Friends and associates—Juvenile literature. 2. William, Prince, grandson of Elizabeth II, Queen of Great Britain, 1982—Relations with women—Juvenile literature. 3. Middleton, Kate, 1982—Relations with men—Juvenile literature. 4. Royal couples—Great Britain— Biography—Juvenile literature. I. Title. II. Title: Prince William and Kate.
    DA591.A45W5553 2012
    941.085092'2—dc22 [B]   2011003413

Manufactured in the United States of America
1 – DP – 7/15/11

CONTENTS

Kate Middleton and Prince William of Wales pose for photographers at a press conference announcing their engagement on November 16, 2010, in London, England. Kate wears the engagement ring William gave her, which belonged to his mother, Princess Diana.

Cameras flashed and reporters buzzed. Prince William of Wales and Kate Middleton walked across the floor of St. James's Palace in London, England. William was dressed in a dark suit. Kate wore a bright blue dress.

The couple was announcing their engagement to be married. It was the biggest news to come out of the British royal family in years. Prince William is in line to become king one day. Kate will possibly become a future queen.

The couple spoke to the press. Kate showed off the engagement ring William had given her. The diamond and sapphire ring had belonged to his famous mother, Princess Diana. "This was my way of making sure that my mother didn't miss out on today," William told reporters.

William and Kate had known each other for nine years. Their relationship had survived many ups and downs. But they were finally ready to be married. And they weren't the only ones excited. People around the world couldn't wait to see what kind of storybook wedding the couple had planned.

Born to Be King

William Arthur Philip Louis of Wales was born June 21, 1982, in London, England. William's birth was big news. His parents were the famous Charles and Diana, Prince and Princess of Wales. Little William's grandmother was Queen Elizabeth II. That made William second in line, behind his father, to become Britain's king one day. His formal title was His Royal Highness Prince William of Wales.

Diana, who had not been born into royalty, wanted William and his younger brother, Harry (born in 1984), to have normal childhood experiences. She protected

Princess Diana and Prince Charles leave St. Mary's Hospital with baby Prince William in June 1982.

Diana *(back row)*, William *(front row, left),* and Harry *(front row, right)* enjoy a ride at Disney World during a Florida vacation.

them from the press. She exposed them to both the good and the bad in life. The children went to Disney World. But they also visited homeless shelters and hospitals. They went to public parks where the boys played with the children of nonroyals. Diana wanted her young princes to understand the lives of people of all backgrounds.

Diana herself was hounded by the press. Pesky photographers called paparazzi followed her every move. The constant attention often left her depressed. On at

Being followed by paparazzi was a way of life for Diana. She and Charles tried to shield their sons from the same treatment.

least one occasion, she had threatened to take her own life. Young William decided that he wanted to protect his mother. When he was ten years old, he told her, "When I grow up, I want to be a policeman and look after you." To that, little Harry responded, "Oh no, you can't. You've got to be king."

William—affectionately called Wills by friends and family—was well aware of his destiny. As a child, he got into more than his share of mischief. Once he was sent home from a friend's birthday party after throwing a tantrum because he couldn't blow out the candles on the cake. But as he grew older, he became a well-behaved young man. Those close to him described him as being perceptive (able to see and understand things clearly) and generous. He seemed to grasp the kind of personality he would need to have as king. Although the public

Left to right: Charles, Harry, William, and Diana go for a bicycle ride on a family vacation in 1989. The public loved to see photos of the royal family.

got only short glimpses of the young man, he enjoyed incredible popularity.

The royal family couldn't just send William to any school. He had to have the best education, and he had to be protected from the press. From preschool onward, he attended small, private schools, including Wetherby School in London and Ludgrove in Wokingham, west of London. In 1995 he started secondary school (high school) at Eton College, an all-boys school. The school wasn't far from one of his royal grandmother's homes, Windsor Castle.

King of What?

So what exactly might William be king of one day? This simple question has a complicated answer.

The ruling monarch (king or queen) is the formal head of state for sixteen nations known as the Commonwealth Realms. These include the United Kingdom, Australia, Canada, New Zealand, and others. He or she is also the figurehead (leader without real power) of the Commonwealth of Nations, which includes fifty-four nations, all but two of which were once a part of the huge British Empire. Finally, the monarch is the symbolic leader of the Church of England.

Centuries ago, the monarch held real power. He or she could make and enforce laws. That's no longer true, but the monarch does have some political power. Monarchs can direct attention to important issues. They also can play a key role in international diplomacy (dealings between nations).

William's grandmother, Queen Elizabeth II, lives in Buckingham Palace with her husband, Prince Philip.

Reporters and photographers could have made high school a very difficult time for William. But his family made a deal with the press. If the press left him alone, the family would give them regular updates about his life. And so William was allowed to live his teenage years with some small bit of privacy.

William was busy at Eton. He was popular and got good grades, although a few subjects, such as biology, proved difficult for him. William was also a good athlete. He enjoyed playing sports of all kinds and excelled at swimming, water polo, basketball, and soccer. He was captain of his school's soccer team. Life was good. But everything was about to change.

William enjoyed participating in many sports at Eton College, including soccer.

Overcoming Tragedy

In 1996 Charles and Diana announced that they were divorcing. The news was not a big surprise. The couple had been having marital problems for years. But things would soon get much worse for William.

In August 1997, the two princes had just returned from a stay in southern France with their mother. After the vacation, Diana went back to Paris, France. On August 31, she was killed in a car crash. The boys were in Scotland with their father. Charles woke William, aged fifteen, and Harry, twelve, to tell them the terrible news that their mother was dead.

Rumors swirled about Diana's death. She and two others were killed in the accident. Many people blamed the crash on the paparazzi, who were following Diana in hopes of snapping some photos. The blame was later placed on the carelessness of the driver of Diana's car. But

The car crash that killed Diana, along with two others, in Paris, France, in 1997 was later blamed on the car's driver.

the paparazzi's role in her death fueled a growing dislike William had for the media (newspapers, TV, and other mass-communication sources).

Millions of people around the world watched Diana's funeral on TV. Among the most touching scenes was that of young William and Harry walking behind their mother's casket as she was carried to her final resting place.

Left to right: Prince Philip, William's grandfather; William; Charles Spencer, Diana's brother; Harry; and Charles walk behind the casket during the funeral procession for Diana in London in September 1997.

Bouquets from the British people are piled in front of Kensington Palace in London, where Diana lived. The country shared William's grief over his mother's death.

At the time, the princes were sheltered from the media. But years later, William described his feelings. "Initially there is a sense of profound shock and disbelief that this could ever happen to you," he said. "Real grief often does not hit home until much later. For many it is a grief never entirely lost. Life is altered as you know it, and not a day goes past without you thinking about the one you have lost."

The following summer, William celebrated his sixteenth birthday. He was growing into a strong and handsome young man. He had become something of a heartthrob among teenaged girls. His photograph appeared on teen magazine covers. *People* magazine included him on their list of the Most Beautiful People of 1998.

In 2000 William graduated from Eton. Rather than move straight on to a university, he took a year off to travel. This practice, called taking a gap year, is common among British students. William headed to South America. There, he took part in exercises with the British Army. He also spent time teaching children in a poor community in Chile. As a teacher, he had to do all sorts of chores. Most famously, a photographer snapped a picture of the future king cleaning a toilet!

In 2001 it was time to return to formal education. William enrolled at the University of St. Andrews in Scotland. He planned to study art history. Immediately, enrollment applications for female students skyrocketed

William took a year off from his studies between finishing high school and starting college. He spent some of that year working at a school in a village in southern Chile. He not only taught students English but also cleaned bathrooms.

at the university. Lots of young women were hoping to catch the prince's eye!

As chance would have it, a fellow art history major named Kate Middleton did exactly that.

Young Kate

Catherine Elizabeth Middleton—better known as Kate—was born January 9, 1982. She was the first child of Carole and Michael, a middle-class couple who had met when both were working in the airline industry. Kate's family later grew with a sister, Pippa, and a brother, James. The family lived in Bucklebury, Berkshire, about 35 miles (56 kilometers) west of London.

During Kate's early childhood, the family was comfortable but by no means wealthy. In 1987 Carole and Michael started a party supply business called Party Pieces. The company

Three-year-old Kate climbs a rock in England's Lake District in 1986.

Kate's parents, Michael and Carole Middleton (shown here in 2010), started a successful party supply business when Kate was young.

sent out catalogs advertising their products. Many of the photographs featured young Kate and Pippa. The business grew into a success, and the family soon became millionaires.

The money allowed Carole and Michael to give their children the best possible education. Kate went to the nearby St. Andrew's School, an exclusive and expensive private school. There, Kate was well liked and active. She participated in public speaking and debate events. She performed in school plays. And like William, she was an athlete. She swam, played tennis, hockey, volleyball, and more. She even set the school record for her age group in the high jump. "Kate was very sporty," said a former classmate. "I don't think there was a sport she couldn't [excel at]."

Kate graduated from St. Andrew's School in 1995. Next, she spent a short time at an all-girls boarding school called Downe House. In early 1996, she switched to a different boarding school named Marlborough College. Marlborough is west of Berkshire and has both boys and

Kate *(center)* played sports at St. Andrew's School and later at Marlborough College. She always made a point of welcoming new girls, remembering her own difficulty in adjusting to the school.

girls as students. Living away from home was a big change. Kate, aged fourteen, was shy at first. It was hard joining a new school during the middle of a term. According to one report, the boys at the school made a practice of "rating" the girls' looks on a scale of 1 to 10. Kate got mostly ones and twos. Her friends said that she was unsure of herself and very lacking in confidence. Her social difficulties and terrible homesickness made this a hard time in her life.

Soon, Kate made friends. They called her Middle-bum, a play on her last name. But it was in fun. Kate quickly became popular and was described as sweet, loyal, and hardworking. She always made a point of welcoming new girls to the school, because of her own difficulty in adjusting.

By 1998 the lanky, awkward Kate had grown into a young woman who got a lot of attention from boys. "It happened quite suddenly," her friend Gemma Williamson said of the transformation. "Catherine came back after the long summer break the following year an absolute beauty. . . . She just had an innate sense of style." Her friends teased her about it, calling her Princess in

Kate *(left)* and her friend Gemma Williamson *(right)* attended Marlborough College together. They are shown here in 2000, their last year at the school.

Waiting, even though she had never met Prince William. In truth, the nickname wasn't that remarkable. Just about every sixteen-year-old schoolgirl in Great Britain fantasized about one day marrying the prince.

In 2000 Kate graduated from Marlborough. Like William, she took a gap year. Kate traveled to Italy, where she studied the country's language and art. She also went to the island of Barbados on a family vacation. In the fall of 2001, Kate's gap year was over and she started her first term at the University of St. Andrews, where she would study art history.

The University of St. Andrews

The University of St. Andrews in Saint Andrews, Scotland, is the oldest university in Scotland. It was founded in 1413. In the English-speaking world, only the University of Oxford and the University of Cambridge are older. The university's history and tradition are apparent in its old stone buildings and cobblestone walkways.

The modern-day university boasts around nine thousand students from around the world. It is best known as an arts and humanities university. But it also has gained attention for scientific research.

William, Meet Kate

The royal family's agreement with the press continued as William entered St. Andrews. He came to the university in late September 2001. Kate was already settled into her dorm by the time he arrived. At first, William—who lived on another floor of the same dorm as Kate—kept his distance from the rest of the students. He feared disrupting their lives and studies. He declined invitations to clubs and parties.

But in time, his attitude changed. He grew more sociable. He made friends. As a fellow first-year art history major, Kate was one of those early friends. The two discovered that they had a lot in common. Both loved sports and life in the country. They had similar senses of humor. They both enjoyed traveling and swapped stories about their adventures

William was a loner in his first months at St. Andrews. But later, he developed close friendships with many students, including Kate.

Kate, shown at a St. Andrews event in 2001, enjoyed college life. Here she is in the middle of a shaving cream fight.

on their gap years. But the relationship was still just a friendship. William reportedly dated a young actress named Carly Massy-Birch, whom Kate also counted as a friend. Meanwhile, Kate dated twenty-two-year-old law student Rupert Finch.

By December, William and Carly had broken up. William was feeling down and homesick. He questioned whether St. Andrews had been the right choice for him and considered switching to a university closer to home. Prince Charles warned his son that leaving the university would reflect poorly on his character. Many credit Kate's friendship and support with changing his mind. She suggested he switch his major to geography. He took the advice and stuck it out at St. Andrews.

William continued to come out of his shell. He was bothered by students—many of them Americans—following him around and staring. But he soon learned to ignore the unwanted attention. He joined the university's athletics club, where he played rugby, soccer, and water polo.

By the end of the school year, William and Kate were clearly quite close. (Kate's relationship with Rupert had also ended by this time.) They, along with two other friends, planned to share an apartment the following year. Rumors began to swirl that they were romantically attached. The two insisted that they weren't dating, but many people were unconvinced.

His Highness and Her Shyness

William and Kate's actions fueled the rumors that they were a couple. Kate was William's guest at a weekend party in November 2002. In May 2003, they attended a charity ball together. They reportedly spent most of their time together with friends, tucked away in a corner. Shortly thereafter, Kate was on hand to cheer on William in a rugby match. While they never kissed or showed outward affection in public, many thought that their body language suggested a romantic relationship.

In the summer of 2003, reports said that William was involved with Jessica Craig, an old friend. But he quickly put down that rumor by releasing a public statement to deny it. In fact, he denied having any girlfriend. He wrote, "There's been a lot of speculation about every single girl I'm with, and it actually does irritate me after a while, more so because it's a complete pain for the girls."

William and Kate went on a skiing trip to Switzerland together in March 2004. It was the first time the two had been photographed together.

William was trying to protect Kate by hiding their relationship. He knew how the media would hound her and her family once word got out. But by March 2004—with both William and Kate in their junior year at St. Andrews—all doubt about their romance was erased. The two went on a skiing trip together, and a photographer snapped a photo of them together looking cozy. The photograph was printed in newspapers around the world. The secret was out. William and Kate were an item. And no denials came from William or the royal family.

Still, Kate kept a very low profile. She did not talk to the media. She gave no public interviews. She avoided attention whenever possible. Soon the media had a nickname for the couple—His Highness and Her Shyness.

It wasn't all a fairy tale. After their third year at St. Andrews, the media reported that the relationship was in trouble. According to some sources, William had planned a trip to Africa, complete with a visit to Jessica Craig.

Newspapers started writing about a rivalry between Kate and Jessica, calling it the Battle of the Babes. If there truly was such a battle, Kate won it. William never made the trip to Africa. However, the following summer, he did take a trip alone to the United States, and rumors spread about possible romantic entanglements there.

Kate welcomed William back later that summer, and the two returned to St. Andrews for their final year. During this time, Kate spent more time with William's family. She was a hit. She charmed Prince Charles and his fiancée Camilla Parker Bowles. She joked around with Prince Harry. Some people started to wonder if an engagement might be soon coming.

Left to right: Harry; William; Charles; Camilla Parker Bowles; and her children, Laura and Tom, are pictured on Charles and Camilla's wedding day in 2005.

Kate and William look happy on their graduation day from St. Andrews in June 2005.

But William put those questions to rest. One evening in a night-club, William made the uncharacteristic move of talking to a reporter. Asked about a possible marriage, William said, "Look, I'm only 22, for God's sake. . . . I don't want to get married until I'm at least 28, or maybe 30."

That statement, among other things, led to renewed speculation that the romance would soon be ending. Some thought that it was a university romance, due to run its course when the couple graduated. Both finished their final exams on May 25, 2005, and then attended a formal graduation ceremony a month later. Their time at the university was over. A new phase of their lives was beginning.

Choosing Their Paths

Leaving school was a big change for both William and Kate. But Kate, who hadn't grown up in the public eye, was more affected. At St. Andrews, she had been somewhat protected from the media. But that protection was gone. Kate was constantly hounded by the paparazzi. She could barely take a step out in public without cameras flashing in her face. In October, she filed a complaint against the press, saying she had done nothing to warrant such attention. The royal family supported her and asked the media to give her some space. Some newspapers agreed, refusing to publish paparazzi photographs of her, but the harassment didn't stop.

How could the girlfriend of the future king find a normal job? Kate knew it would be a problem. She sent résumés to art galleries. She also worked on plans to begin her own business selling children's clothing on the Internet. But because she had no job and seemed to be just waiting to become a princess, the media started calling her Waity Katie.

Meanwhile, William was mapping out his future. Prince Harry had joined the British Army in 2005, and William decided to follow his brother's lead. In January 2006, he entered the Royal Military Academy Sandhurst. There

Both William *(left)* and Harry *(right),* shown here in 2006, joined the British Army and became officers at Sandhurst.

Kate *(center)* and her brother, James Middleton *(left)*, and mother, Carole Middleton *(right)*, attended William's graduation from Sandhurst in 2006.

he trained to become an army officer. He wanted to become a pilot someday. Harry was already an officer. He couldn't resist taking a jab at his older brother. "I'll have to make a special effort to visit him for comedy value just so he can salute me," Harry joked.

Life at Sandhurst was difficult for William. He was treated like any other cadet (student) at the school. The physical training was intense. He later said that he was often so exhausted that he couldn't get up in time to have his bed made for morning inspection. But he kept at it and was later described as a model cadet.

William graduated from Sandhurst in December 2006. The graduating cadets take part in a graduating ceremony called a passing out parade. Kate was there with William's family—including the queen—to watch him formally receive his army commission. He became Second Lieutenant Wales. Kate didn't give any interviews after the ceremony. But one TV network hired a lip reader to watch her. According to the network, Kate said, "I love the uniform. It's so sexy."

William joined the British Army regiment (group) known as the Blues and Royals. After four more months of training, he became a troop commander.

Meanwhile, Kate had finally found a job. She was a buyer for the retail chain Jigsaw. She helped find fashion accessories that the stores would sell. It was a good fit for Kate, whom many credited with having a great sense of fashion.

Kate's new boss, Belle Robinson, knew that having the famous princess-in-waiting as an employee would be a challenge. "There were days when there were TV crews at the end of the drive," Robinson said. "We'd say, 'Listen, do you want to go out the back way?' And she'd say, 'To be honest, they're going to hound us until they've got the picture. So why don't we just go, get the picture done, and then they'll leave us alone.' I thought she was very mature."

Kate *(left)* has a close relationship with her family, including her sister, Pippa Middleton *(right)*. Family support has made it easier to deal with the press.

Ups and Downs

William was busy with his military career, and the couple spent most of their time apart. The relationship was hitting a rocky patch. Reports said that Kate was pressuring William for a commitment but that the prince wasn't ready to settle down. The media pressure on both of them was building. And then in March 2007, stories surfaced of William behaving badly with his fellow officers at a nightclub. Two women spoke to reporters about William grabbing them, and one incident was caught in a photograph. While no one accused William of actually cheating on Kate, the reports, if true, would have been a huge embarrassment to her.

In April 2007, everything became too much for the couple. They broke up. Their split made headlines worldwide. The couple never disclosed their reason for calling it quits but agreed that the decision was mutual.

William and Kate reacted to the breakup in very different ways. For the first few days, Kate withdrew, avoiding attention. Meanwhile, William seemed determined to be seen having fun. He went to concerts and nightclubs. He behaved wildly and, according to some, made a spectacle of himself.

The media was relentless, following Kate everywhere. Some reporters said that the breakup had come because of Kate's middle-class upbringing. They accused Kate's mother of causing it. William was so bothered by the stories that he called Kate to make sure she knew he wasn't behind them. Kate was offered huge sums of money to tell her story. But she turned down all offers. She wasn't about to give the press what they wanted.

Kate eventually returned to the social scene. Within a week, she was seen in a revealing minidress having drinks with Guy Pelly, one of William's close friends. She was out flirting, dating, and dancing. According to those close to William, the prince was beside himself with jealousy.

William realized his mistake, and within months, the couple was back together. They appeared together at the Concert for Diana on July 1, 2007. The concert was a charity event William and Harry had organized to honor their mother on the tenth anniversary of her death.

Harry and William *(second and third from left, front row)* organized a concert in memory of their mother. Kate was also in attendance *(far right, third row)*.

In December 2007, Harry went to Afghanistan to fight in the war there. Some wondered if William might follow. William had claimed that he was prepared to see action. In an interview, he said, "What's the point of me doing all my training and being there for my guys when I can turn around to somebody and say, 'Well I'm far too important, I'm not going [to war].'"

But the realist in William probably knew that the future king would never be allowed to see combat. And in fact, when his squad was sent to Afghanistan, he was left behind. So he made other plans. He had long dreamed about being a pilot, like his father. So in January 2008, he began training with the Royal Air Force (RAF).

Training to be a pilot was hard work. William spent long days studying. Within a few weeks, he made his first training flight. The plane was a small trainer called a Grob 115E. He later graduated to more advanced planes and then to helicopters. William's training was not without controversy, however. He had long said he didn't want any special treatment in the military. But the press heavily criticized him when he used military aircraft for personal "joyrides." So he did occasionally use his status for a little extra privilege.

William spent most of his free time with Kate. They went on ski trips and attended parties. In April 2008, when William officially received his RAF wings, Kate was there to cheer him on. Meanwhile, Kate had left her job at Jigsaw. She said that she wanted some time

Kate attended the ceremony when William received his Royal Air Force wings in April 2008.

to herself. She spent some of that time studying fashion photography, a field in which she had developed an interest. She also worked on building a catalog for her parents' party planning business.

Countdown to Engagement

When Kate left her job, many people thought an engagement announcement would be coming soon. However, some people—including the queen—thought that Kate's behavior was irresponsible. Britain was in an economic downturn. Queen Elizabeth had a reputation as a hard worker, and she wanted the royal family to share that reputation. Reports surfaced that she had told William to wait on an engagement until Kate could figure out a productive way to spend her time.

While Kate didn't bow to pressure and take a job, she was active with charities, especially the Starlight Children's Foundation. She helped raise money for the charity, which helps terminally ill children.

Meanwhile, William remained focused on his military career. In June 2008, he began training with the Royal Navy. After his training, William served briefly aboard the HMS *Iron Duke*, a navy frigate (ship) in the Caribbean Sea. During this time, William took part in a successful mission to capture a ship carrying illegal drugs. Then, in September, William announced that he would begin training to become an RAF rescue pilot.

"The time I spent with the RAF earlier this year made me realize how much I love flying," he said. "Joining search and rescue is a perfect opportunity for me to serve."

The news that William was remaining in the military pleased some and disappointed others. Many felt it was important that the future king have a military background. Others saw it as little more than a public relations stunt. According to some, Kate was less than pleased with the news. William's career took most of his time and left her still waiting on an engagement that many felt was overdue.

Still, William's mind was made up. He began his training at the Defence Helicopter Flying School in west central England in January 2009. He graduated a year later. In April 2010, he began a tour of duty as a copilot in the RAF's No. 22 Squadron, a search-and-rescue unit

William decided to stay in the military, and he trained to be a search-and-rescue helicopter pilot. He is shown here in 2010.

in Wales that flies a helicopter called the Sea King. In October, William took part in his first rescue. He and three squad mates flew to an off-shore gas rig (mining equipment used to collect natural gas). There, they picked up a worker who had suffered a heart attack and delivered him to a hospital.

Later that month, William and Kate took a vacation to Kenya, Africa. They went to the Lewa Wildlife Conservancy. On October 19, William finally proposed. The couple has not revealed the details of the proposal, but Kate assured the media that it was very romantic. To nobody's surprise, she said yes.

The Future

In November 2010, the couple made their engagement public. Later, they announced that the wedding would take place April 29, 2011. They would wed in a church called Westminster Abbey.

The wedding was a gala affair, with Kate in a beautiful ivory-and-white gown and William in military attire. The couple promised their lives to each other with the whispered words "I will" and left the church in an open carriage.

Kate *(left)* waves to the crowds outside Westminster Abbey in London as she arrives for her wedding to William on April 29, 2011. Her sister, Pippa, the maid of honor, holds the train of her dress.

Top: William wore military attire for the wedding, and Kate wore a wedding gown made for her by a British fashion designer. The tiara she wore was borrowed from the queen. They are seen here outside Westminster Abbey after the ceremony.

Bottom: Kate and William walk down the aisle after the wedding ceremony. Harry, who served as best man, and Pippa walk behind the couple and the children in the wedding party.

Top: Kate and William wave to people lining the street as they ride in a horse-drawn carriage to Buckingham Palace after the wedding ceremony.

Left: Kate and William exchange a kiss on the balcony at Buckingham Palace, a tradition at royal weddings.

Bottom: Prince Charles and Camilla *(far left)* and Queen Elizabeth *(far right)* join the newlyweds on the balcony to wave to the crowds. The queen gave William the title Duke of Cambridge, making Kate Duchess of Cambridge.

What does the future hold for Will and Kate? William's father is in line to become king upon Queen Elizabeth's death, so William will have to wait. If William does one day become king, he will be King William, while Kate will be the Queen Consort (this means that she is the king's wife and not in line to become ruler herself upon his death). She will be called Queen Catherine. But with William's grandmother and father both still alive and healthy, such concerns may be a long way off.

William has no immediate plans to leave RAF service. His tour of duty, which he started in April 2010, will likely last thirty to thirty-six months, and he might continue on after that. He says that he loves flying and enjoys the job. Kate will likely remain active in charities. Some think she has a future working in the world of fashion as well. Every year, she is mentioned on a variety of "best dressed" lists, and she has some experience in the industry.

William and Kate's story has had its share of highs and lows. But the public loves the couple, and they appear to be in love with each other. Many believe that they will one day make an excellent king and queen.

Important Dates

1981   Prince Charles and Princess Diana are married at St. Paul's Cathedral in London.

1982   Kate Middleton is born on January 9. Prince William is born on June 21.

1995   William enrolls at Eton College. Kate enrolls at Downe House.

1996   Charles and Diana are divorced. Kate enrolls at Marlborough College.

1997   After a holiday with William and Harry, Diana is killed in a car accident. The young princes attend their mother's funeral.

2000   William and Kate both graduate from secondary school. William begins his gap year in South America. Kate spends her gap year in Italy.

2001   William and Kate enroll at the University of St. Andrews, where they meet. In December, William thinks about leaving the university, but Kate helps to talk him out of it.

2002	Rumors begin to circulate that William and Kate are a couple. They agree to be housemates for their second year at St. Andrews.
2004	William and Kate are photographed skiing together, erasing all doubt that they are a couple.
2005	In June, William and Kate graduate from St. Andrews.
2006	William joins the army and trains at the Royal Military Academy Sandhurst. Kate finds a job as an accessories buyer for the retail chain Jigsaw. She is on hand to see William graduate from Sandhurst in December.
2007	In April, William and Kate break up. They are back together within a few months and attend the Concert for Diana on July 1. In December, Kate quits her job at Jigsaw.
2008	William begins pilot training with the Royal Air Force (RAF). That summer he serves aboard a Royal Navy frigate. Kate helps with her parents' business, volunteers for charities, and studies photography.

2009	William begins training to become a search-and-rescue pilot for the RAF.
2010	In April, William begins a tour of duty in Wales with the RAF. He takes part in his first rescue in October. Later that month, on a trip to Africa, he proposes to Kate. The couple announce their engagement in November.
2011	The royal wedding takes place on April 29 in Westminster Abbey.

Source Notes

7   Melissa Castellanos, "Kate Middleton's Engagement Ring Is Princess Diana's," cbsnews.com, November 16, 2010, http://www.cbsnews.com/8301-31749_162-20022950-10391698.html (April 19, 2011).

10 Andrew Morton, *Diana: Her True Story in Her Own Words* (New York: Pocket Books, 1998), 293.

16 Philippe Naughton, "Diana's Death Made Mummy a 'Hollow Word', Says William," *Times Online*, March 13, 2009, http://www.timesonline.co.uk/tol/news/uk/article5900342.ece (April 19, 2011).

19   Claudia Joseph, *Kate: Kate Middleton; Princess in Waiting* (New York: Avon, 2009), 125.

21   Ibid., 135.

25   Ibid., 165.

28   Ibid.

30   Katie Nicholl, *William and Harry: Behind the Palace Walls* (London, Preface Publishing, 2010), 98.

30   Joseph, *Kate*, 199.

31   Ibid., 209-210.

34   Nicholl, *William and Harry*, 137.

36   Simon Perry, "Prince William Chooses Full-Time Military Career," *People*, September 15, 2008, http://www.people.com/people/article/0,,20225736,00.html (April 19, 2011).

Selected Bibliography

Graham, Tim, and Peter Archer. *HRH Prince William of Wales.* London: Simon & Schuster, 2003.

——. *Jubilee: A Celebration of 50 Years of the Reign of Her Majesty Queen Elizabeth II.* London: Cassell, 2002.

Hoey, Brian. *Prince William.* Phoenix Mill, UK: Sutton, 2003.

Joseph, Claudia. *Kate: Kate Middleton; Princess in Waiting.* New York: Avon, 2009.

Morton, Andrew. *Diana: Her True Story in Her Own Words*. New York: Pocket Books, 1998.

Nicholl, Katie. *William and Harry: Behind the Palace Walls*. London: Preface Publishing, 2010.

Simmons, Simone, and Ingrid Seward. *Diana: The Last Word*. New York: St. Martin's Press, 2005.

Further Reading

BOOKS

Hajeski, Nancy. *Princesses*. New York: Hammond World Atlas, 2009.

Krohn, Katherine. *Princess Diana*. Minneapolis: Twenty-First Century Books, 1998.

Landau, Elaine. *Prince William: WOW: William of Wales*. Minneapolis: Lerner Publications Company, 2002.

Mattern, Joanne. *Princess Diana*. New York: DK, 2006.

Paprocki, Sherry Beck. *Diana, Princess of Wales: Humanitarian*. New York: Chelsea House, 2009.

Roshell, Starshine. *Real-Life Royalty*. Mankato, MN: Child's World, 2008.

WEBSITES

How Royalty Works

http://www.howstuffworks.com/royalty.htm
Learn more about royalty around the world, how royal families come into power, and what rules govern the passing of that power from generation to generation.

Princess Diana Biography

http://www.biography.com/articles/Princess-Diana-9273782
Biography.com hosts this brief biography of Princess Diana. Read more about her life or watch a short video. The page also links to the biographies of other royals, including Prince William.

Prince William

http://www.royal.gov.uk/ThecurrentRoyalFamily/
PrinceWilliam/PrinceWilliam.aspx
This is Prince William's page on the official website of the British monarchy. It includes a biography, photo gallery, and links to other members of the royal family.

The Royal Wedding

http://www.officialroyalwedding2011.org/
View the special day and its events at this site.

William and Kate

http://www.williamkate.com
Check out this site for all the latest news on the royal couple. Read news clips from around the world, see photos of the couple, and more.

Index